GABRIEL FAURE

Requiem

OPUS 48

for soprano & baritone soli,
SATB & orchestra

Edited with piano accompaniment
by Desmond Ratcliffe

vocal score

Order No: NOV 072304

NOVELLO

EDITORIAL NOTE

Sources consulted

Paris, Bibliothèque Nationale, autograph score. The scoring is as follows:

Introit—Kyrie SATB, strings (without violins) and organ, with imprecise annotations of horns and trumpets.

Sanctus SATB, 2 bassoons, 4 horns, 2 trumpets, harp, strings and organ.

Agnus Dei SATB, 2 bassoons, 4 horns, strings (without violins) and organ. Some bars for harp have been deleted.

In Paradisum SATB, 2 bassoons, harp, strings and organ.

The *Offertorium*, *Pie Jesu* and *Libera me* are missing.

Paris, J. Hamelle, complete printed edition of 1900.

Square brackets have been used to denote editorial additions; dynamics have been adjusted on a logical basis and errors corrected. Occasional small notes in the piano reduction are a guide to the part-writing and not necessarily playable.

Grateful acknowledgement is made to the Department of Music, Bibliothèque Nationale, Paris, for supplying a microfilm of the manuscript for the purposes of this edition.

D.R. 1975

ORCHESTRATION

2 Flutes
2 Clarinets in B flat
2 Bassoons

4 Horns in F
2 Trumpets in F
3 Trombones

Timpani (2)

Harp

Strings

Organ

Full Score and Parts are available on hire.

DURATION ABOUT 40 MINUTES

CONTENTS

REQUIEM

Edited with piano accompaniment
by Desmond Ratcliffe

GABRIEL FAURE
Opus 48

I INTROIT - KYRIE

© *Novello & Company Limited 1975*

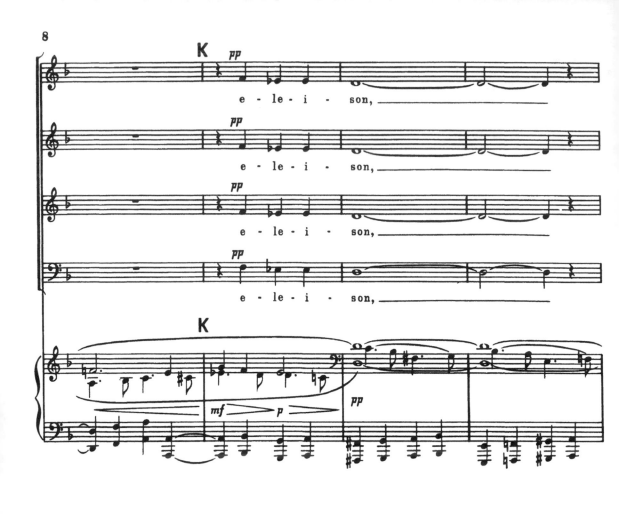

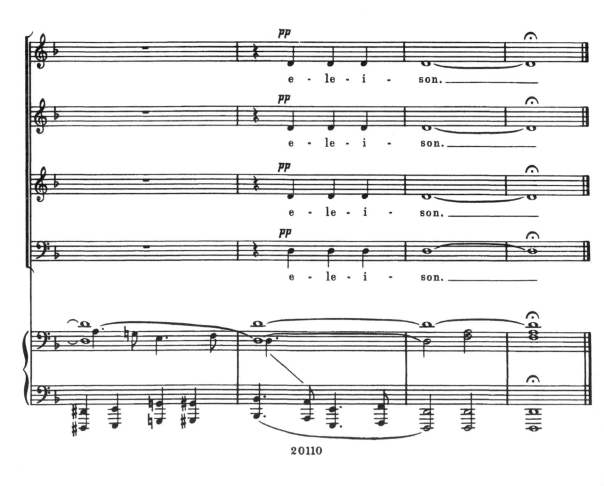

II OFFERTORIUM

poe - nis in - fer - ni, de poe - nis in - fer - ni, et de pro -
poe - nis in - fer - ni, de poe - nis in - fer - ni, et de pro -
poe - nis in - fer - ni, de poe - nis in - fer - ni, et de pro -
to - rum de poe - nis in - fer - ni, et de pro -

fun - do la - cu:___ ne ca - dant in obs - cu -
fun - do la - cu:___ ne ca - dant in obs - cu -
fun - do la - cu:___ ne ca - dant in obs - cu -
fun - do la - cu:___ ne ca - dant in obs - cu -

III SANCTUS

IV PIE JESU

V AGNUS DEI

VI LIBERA ME

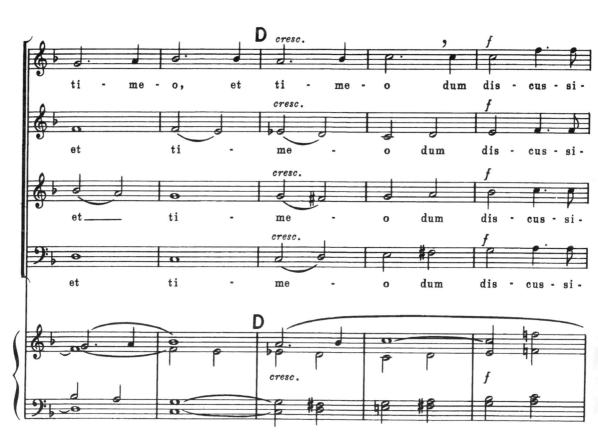

VII IN PARADISUM